Argument
Love, Wealth And Spirituality

by

Rina Roy

Double9 BOOKS

Argument

Love, Wealth And Spirituality

by Rina Roy

ISBN: 978-93-64286-10-7

Published by

DOUBLE 9 BOOKS

2/13-B, Ansari Road
Daryaganj, New Delhi – 110002
info@double9books.com
www.double9books.com
Tel. 011-40042856

ABOUT THE AUTHOR

"Rina Roy, a final-year MA student in English Literature at JNRM College, Port Blair, resides on the tranquil island of Little Andaman in the Andaman and Nicobar Islands. Raised amidst the challenges of her father's farming and the nurturing care of her parents, Rina credits her mother as a luminous figure in her life, describing her as an angel who sacrificed her own happiness to illuminate her daughter's path. Grateful for her upbringing, Rina cherishes her parents' unwavering support, likening their care to that of handling a delicate wax doll.

Reflecting on her journey, Rina acknowledges the influence of numerous individuals, but none more profoundly than Kusum Ma'am, her mentor and guide. Kusum Ma'am not only enriched her academic pursuits but also imparted invaluable life lessons, igniting Rina's passion for storytelling and literature. Inspired by Kusum Ma'am's mentorship, Rina now embarks on her first literary endeavor, a testament to her burgeoning love for writing.

With determination and gratitude, Rina strives to craft a compelling narrative that resonates with readers, hoping her work finds appreciation among its audience. Driven by her ambition and supported by her cherished memories and teachings, Rina remains steadfast in her pursuit of literary success, acknowledging the challenges yet unwavering in her commitment to excellence.Rina's love for literature extends beyond writing; she finds joy in collecting books from various genres and eras, continues to grow as a write. She influence to started writing to her own writings after reading a few pages of the Bhagavad Gita"

CONTENTS

Dedicated to the love,
wealth
and
spirituality

Preface

When I was reading related something about mythology, I thought that like that just as we human have fights one love, differences health and spirituality. So, they were God then such things must have happened in them too keeping this is my mind, some thought started coming to my mind and thinking about it deeply, I wrote this short fictional story about mythology. Well in this story I have shown how Narayan ji has the feeling of strength and one.

How does he defeat the enemy and conquer love with his beloved. On the other hand, Goddess Lakshmi ji handles the burden of fame and wealth of entire world and also how she quarrels with her love. This entire book talks about love, anger and spirituality of Narayan ji and wealth, power, and culture of Lakshmi ji.

ACKNOWLEDGEMENT

This book is the fictional mythology story of the goddess Narayan and his beloved God of wealth Lakshmi ji The Idea of hesitating this story comes from the reading of Hindu mythology which encompasses a vast collection of ancient texts, sculptures and stories that have been passed down legends are found in various Hindu religious texts such as Upanishads epics Vedas, Mahabharata and Ramayana.

Specifically, the stories of lord Narayan and goddess Lakshmi can be found in texts like the Vishnu Purana, Bhagavata Purana and other puranic texts. The goddess Narayanan and Lakshmi seek their blessings for protection, prosperity and spiritual fulfillment.

I am grateful fora number of friends Ritesh Mondal (Bengal Fine Arts College) [Sujata Das, Rumpa Halder. {MA English} from JNRM College PORT BLAIR, thankful for helping me to decorate the book]. And my dear teacher [Dr. Kusum Kumari Professor of English Department JNRM College] -

Thanks to inspired and encouraging me to start the work, preserve with it and to publish it. Finally, I would like to acknowledge with gratitude the support and love of my near once my friend's family. They all kept me going and this book would not have been possible with them.

I

Once upon a time there was a dream King named Hiranyakashipu who wanted to be immortal and rule over the entire universe. He was granted a boon that made him nearly invincible. However, his son Prahlada was a devoted follower of Narayana.

Hiranyakashipu tried to kill Prahlada, but Narayana protected him at every step finally Narayana protected him at every step finally Narayana appeared in the form of Narsimha a half lion, half human creature and defeated Hirankashyapa restoring peace and righteousness. Everything in the world takes precedence before the truth.

Therefore, be with the truth at every opportunity, God will definitely support you somewhere or somehow, somewhere or the other, when we do something wrong, our inner voice is definitely loud from within, so don't ignore the voice try to understand the right things in yourself which one is thought you right, wrong, true, false and your mistake which you do in your future or present.

From both sides of Narayanas love and anger sides are the both fascinating aspects of his divine nature on one hand Narayana is known for his boundless love compassion and grace towards his devotes. He showers them with blessings, guidance and protection always ready to offer solace and support.

On the other hand, when faced with evil or injustice, Narayana can display his anger and wrath ensuring that rightness prevails. This duality showcases the multifaced nature of Narayana, where his love and anger coexist to maintain balance in the universe.

Some such history of unique love story of Narayana his beloved. Once upon a time Narayana had an argument with his love Lakshmi over the importance of wealth and material possessions versus spiritual virtues and is the goddess of wealth and prosperity. Express her belief that material wealth is essential for happiness and well - being. On the other hand,

Narayana emphasis the importance of inner virtues such as compassion, humanity and devotion to achieve true fulfillment.

There was a fictional argument and the argument between Narayana and Lakshmi higlights the eternel debate between materialism and sprituality, and the need to strike a balance between the two in life.

It is about time when something happened that there was a difference of opinion between the two beloved. There came a time when both of them started argumenting over some issue. How did it happen why did it happen, there is a no news and no ideas.

Then a quarrel started between the two and there was no end to it. After some time, while fighting, both of them start considering their talent superior to the other and start saying that one has more strength and talent than the other.

Soon, both of them started argument over many issues like, love, lifestyle, intelligence, ownership of house and other related matters. Then their beloved started telling him that everyone is happy with money and wealth, that is the first place in today's time, then Narayana said, wealth and prosperity alone are not everything there should be something which bind the householder together and it is called the bond of love, we can't do this just with money. We have to trust each other, but despite understanding so many things, women stil do not even bother to understanding nor do they try to understand. Since that time, the tradition has been coming that time, the tradition has been coming that women are masters of their own will, they will not be understanding until something happens and no one will be able to stop them until something happen.

Similarly, something similar happened here too. It was proving difficult for Naryanji to understand his lover and his better half. The rest of the gods started thinking that if this continues then no one will agree with anyone because both were right in their own places.

As Narayna ji has said, wealth and fame are important in life but unity is important to get a house to home. Similarly, his beloved god of money and wealth keeping in mind today's way of life, says that unity is important but the first wealth is fame. If you have wealth then everyone lives together, otherwise there would be no one, no one to care for you. After a long topic continues anyway both were right in their place. Like there is a saying that if you are giving a number like nine and you are asked to someone your friend to look at the number from the other side and the opposite side of yourself, then According to the other person it will be called a number six. Similarly, both are correct just need to change the place and the situation of the viewers.

II

In the same way, everyone should try to understand the thinking and feeling of others rather than going beyond their own situation. We should never prove anyone's point of view wrong. Our own way of thinking is not always right, sometimes it is important to understand their too. No one can understand what the other person is going through, everything is not difficult, it is a task which is impossible, only we can try to understand and sympathized others. Both of them Narayan and his beloved talking and argument the other gods decided that if both of them do this, what will happen to everyone and others?

Narayan ji's wife becomes a 'Lotus' out of anger and falls into Narayan's hands because she loves him very much and does not want to go away from him even after a arguments. She could sit away if she wanted but her love doesn't let her separate from him. And Narayan ji also loves her so much that he holds her very tightly so that his love is as strong as it is.

Narayanji wanted the strength of his trust to never break; hence he was holding her tightly, but his beloved started thinking that she held him tightly so that he could capture her and be able to tell his strength. Taking advantage of this situation, 'god of wind' thought of ending their argument, how to change the thinking of both of them by ending the argument and turning into love? He made a plan with some other gods and the help of them He create magical storm. So, that both need each other's support to stable and know that both need each other. Just like in human life no matter how much wealth you earn, there comes a time when you definitely need a life partners. That partner will stand by you in every situation and that partner should be such that when every difficult moment comes, she says don't be afraid, I will be with you in every possible and impossible situation we will lose together and will win together. Anyone who has someone like this in their life is priceless don't let them lose you and you don't lose them. By considering these things god of wind create a storm to that both of them understand each other's importance and not measuring each other's strength.

At first something happened that the lotus made endless efforts to get out of the hands but Naraynji had so much faith in his love that he would hold her with his strength. Narayanji was thinking that something might be happen to lotus and he wanted to protect her at all costs. The continued for a long time and after some time lotus realized that are something is incomplete without strength Lakshmi ji realize that it is not just money but love along with the money that is necessary to run the house become home.

As our emotional attachment, a house is a physical structure or building that provides shelter and serves as a place to live; it is physically made up of rooms, wall, a roof, and other structural elements. And on the other hand a home is more than just a physical space mentally it is a place where one feels comfortable, safe, and at peace.

A home is where one's personal belongings are kept, where memories are made, and where one can relax and be themselves. It is a place of emotional connection and belonging of attachment and the biggest thing where you get the real happiness with your family members.

"Just as to run a household, one needs a preparer and another earner too''.

There comes a time in everyone's life when you have to give up your stubbornness and accept the reality. Therefore, being doing anything, need to think and understand the positive as well as the negative impact once before taking any step.

If the lotus had been accepted at that time before it was formed then the ''Wind God'' not have needed the storm unnecessarily because of the unwanted storm how many things would have been damaged due to those two.

III

To do this that is why the calm sea had to make waves without any proper reason. Because of this the people living on the sea shore would have been frightened and there would have been a commotion among them.

The sea is included in all these things because our deeply impressed devotion and reverence respected Narayan ji and his better half lived in themiddle of the sea.

A golden soft extraordinary snake which had not only one but have seven heads. The appearance of the snake was such that if it came in front of you. You would be stunned you can only imagine its color which is a symbol of love and affection towards Narayan.

According to the Hindu Mythology, the **Serpent Ananta Shesha** also known as **Adi- Shesha or Ananta** is often depicted as a symbol of infinity and eternity. Ananta Shesha is believed to be a thousand - headed Serpent that serve as bed or couch of Lord Narayana as well Lord Vishnu one of the principal duties in Hinduism. The Serpent is said to float on the cosmic waters and support the entire universe. The gesture associated with the snake of Narayan is often depicted in Hindu art iconography. The Serpent is shown coiled around lord Narayan's body with its multiple heads fanning out behind him. This image symbolizes protection, support, and the eternal nature of the universe.

The practice of loving and protecting is something like the Adi- Shesha does to Narayanji. Both of them were together like a shadow of each other.

In some depictions, lord Narayanis shown reclining on the coils of Ananta Shesha with the serpent's hoods forming a protective canopy over his head. This gesture conveys the idea that Narayan is the ultimate source of creation and sustains the universe.

The snake of Narayan represents the idea of cosmic balance, protection, and eternal support provided by the divine forces in Hindu mythology.

Ananta Shesha, also known as a Shesha or Adishesha in a divine serpent and the eternal companion of Lord Narayan Ananta Shesha is said to have infinite heads and is believed to support the entire universe on his believed to support the entire universe on his hoods while floating on the cosmic ocean as the cosmic serpents, Ananta Shesha symbolizes timelessness, eternity and the infinite nature of the universe.

The moment of Ananta Shesha in Hindu mythology represents his role as the bed or seat of Narayana. It is said Narayan reclines on the coils of Ananta Shesha in the cosmic Ocean during the period of cosmic dissolution (Pralaya) between the cycles of creation.

This moment captures the eternal and unchanging aspect of Ananta Shesha as the foundation and support of the universe, as well as his close connection with Lord Narayan as his loyal companion and protector.

"You have a right to perform your prescribed duties, but you are not entitled to the fruits of youraction".

(Bhagavad Gita, Chap.2, Verse47)

Responsibility is the moral obligation to act ethically and be accountable for one's actions, decisions, and their consequences. It involves being reliable, trustworthy, and mindful of the impact one has on others and the environment. To become a responsible person, one must cultivate self-awareness, empathy, and integrity. This entails recognizing one's duties and obligations in various roles, such as a family member, friend, citizen, or professional. Additionally, taking ownership of mistakes, learning from them, and striving to improve are essential aspects of responsible behavior. Developing good communication skills, time management, and prioritization are also crucial for fulfilling commitments and meeting deadlines. Ultimately, being responsible requires a combination of self-discipline, conscientiousness, and a genuine desire to contribute positively to society. Responsibility is a multifaceted concept that encompasses various dimensions of ethical behavior, accountability, and integrity. At its core, responsibility involves acknowledging the impact of one's actions on oneself, others, and the environment, and taking appropriate measures to ensure that those impacts are positive or at least not harmful. It requires a willingness to adhere to moral principles and fulfill obligations, even when it may be challenging or inconvenient. Responsible individuals demonstrate reliability, consistency, and dependability in their words and actions, earning the trust and respect of those around them. They are mindful of the consequences of their choices and strive to make decisions that align with their values and principles.

Becoming a responsible person is a journey that requires self-reflection, self- discipline, and continuous growth. One of the first steps towards cultivating responsibility is developing self- awareness, which involves understanding one's strengths, weaknesses, values, and beliefs. By gaining insight into their own motivations and behaviors, individuals can make more informed choices and take responsibility for the outcomes of those choices. Additionally, empathy plays a crucial role in responsibility, as it allows individuals to consider the perspectives and needs of others, fostering a sense of interconnectedness and mutual respect.

Integrity is another cornerstone of responsibility, as it involves adhering to moral and ethical principles even when faced with adversity or temptation. Acting with integrity means being honest, principled, and transparent in all dealings, both personal and professional. It requires courage and conviction to stand up for what is right, even in the face of opposition or criticism. Furthermore, responsible individuals demonstrate accountability by owning up to their mistakes, learning from them, and taking steps to rectify any harm caused. Rather than making excuses or shifting blame onto others, they take proactive measures to address the consequences of their actions and prevent similar mistakes in the future.

Effective communication skills are essential for fulfilling responsibilities, as they enable individuals to convey their intentions, expectations, and concerns clearly and effectively. Whether in personal relationships, professional settings, or civic engagements, clear communication fosters mutual understanding and collaboration, reducing the likelihood of misunderstandings or conflicts. Additionally, responsible individuals prioritize time management and organization, recognizing the importance of honoring commitments and meeting deadlines. By setting realistic goals, prioritizing tasks, and managing their time effectively, they are better able to fulfill their obligations and make meaningful contributions to their communities.

If an individual chooses to rely solely on faith in God for everything in their life, their actions and experiences may be shaped by their religious beliefs and practices. They may prioritize prayer, worship, and seeking guidance from religious texts or leaders to navigate life's challenges and decisions. Trusting in God's providence, they may believe that their needs will be met and that they will be protected from harm.

In their daily life, they may strive to live according to the teachings of their faith, practicing virtues such as compassion, forgiveness, and generosity. They may also see their experiences, both positive and negative, as opportunities for spiritual growth and learning. Rather than relying solely on their own abilities or resources, they may entrust their fate to God's will, believing that He will guide them and provide for them in accordance with His divine plan.

It's important to note that while faith can provide comfort, strength, and guidance, it does not absolve individuals of personal responsibility or agency. Even those who have faith in God are called to actively engage with the world and make choices that align with their beliefs and values. This may involve taking practical steps to pursue their goals, contribute to their communities, and address challenges they encounter.

In times of difficulty or adversity, individuals who place their faith in God may find solace and support in prayer and in the belief that they are not alone in their struggles. They may also draw strength from the sense of purpose and meaning that their faith provides, trusting that God has a plan for their life and will ultimately bring about good from even the most difficult circumstances.

Ultimately, the ways in which God "saves" individuals who rely on faith alone can vary greatly, as they depend on the individual's beliefs, experiences, and understanding of divine intervention. Some may experience tangible forms of assistance or protection, while others may find comfort and guidance in their faith that helps them navigate life's challenges with resilience and hope.

When an individual chooses to place their faith solely in God, their entire outlook on life can be deeply influenced by their religious beliefs. They may see God as their ultimate provider, protector, and guide, believing that He is present in every aspect of their lives. This profound trust in God's sovereignty can shape their decisions, behaviors, and attitudes in profound ways.

In practical terms, a person who relies solely on faith in God may approach life with a profound sense of humility and surrender. They may recognize their own limitations and acknowledge that they are ultimately dependent on God for everything they have and everything they are. This humility can lead to a greater willingness to seek God's will in all things and to trust in His wisdom, even when it may not align with their own desires or expectations.

Living a life of faith often involves a deep commitment to prayer and spiritual practices. Individuals may devote time each day to prayer, meditation, or reading sacred texts, seeking guidance and inspiration from their religious traditions. These spiritual disciplines can provide a sense of connection to God and a source of strength and comfort in times of difficulty or uncertainty.

In addition to prayer and spiritual practices, individuals who place their faith in God may also cultivate virtues such as patience, perseverance, and compassion. They may strive to live with integrity and to treat others with kindness and respect, recognizing that all people are valued and loved by God.

When faced with challenges or obstacles, individuals who rely on faith in God may turn to Him for help and guidance. They may trust that God is present with them in their struggles and that He has a plan to bring about good, even in the midst of adversity. This trust can provide a source of hope and resilience, enabling them to persevere through difficult times with a sense of peace and assurance.

Ultimately, living a life of faith involves an ongoing journey of trust and obedience, as individuals seek to align their lives with God's will and to live in accordance with their religious beliefs. While faith does not guarantee a life free from suffering or hardship, it can provide a deep sense of meaning, purpose, and connection to something greater than oneself.

In Hindu mythology, Lord Narayana, also known as Vishnu, is revered as the preserver of the universe and the embodiment of compassion and divine grace. Devotees believe that Lord Narayana is ever-present and actively involved in the lives of his devotees, offering guidance, protection, and support in times of need.

One way in which Lord Narayana helps his disciples is through the power of prayer and devotion. Devotees believe that sincere prayers offered to Lord Narayana with faith and devotion can invoke his blessings and assistance. Through prayer, devotees can seek guidance, strength, and protection from Lord Narayana, trusting in his divine wisdom and compassion to help them navigate life's challenges and overcome obstacles.

Devotees also believe that Lord Narayana intervenes in their lives in subtle ways, guiding them towards paths that are in alignment with their spiritual growth and well-being. This divine guidance may manifest as intuitive insights, synchronicities, or unexpected opportunities that seem to arise at just the right moment. Devotees who are attuned to these signs and signals may experience a sense of reassurance and confidence in Lord Narayana's presence and guidance in their lives.

Furthermore, devotees believe that Lord Narayana protects them from harm and adversity, both seen and unseen. They trust in his divine protection to shield them from danger, illness, and misfortune, knowing that he is watching over them with love and compassion. In times of distress or danger, devotees often turn to Lord Narayana for refuge and protection, seeking solace in the belief that he is their ultimate guardian and protector.

Ultimately, the ways in which Lord Narayana helps his disciples to overcome challenges and navigate life's ups and downs are deeply rooted in the bonds of love and devotion between the devotee and the divine. Through prayer, faith, and surrender to his divine will, devotees trust in Lord Narayana's infinite compassion and grace to guide them on their spiritual journey and lead them towards liberation and ultimate union with the divine.

In addition to the spiritual and metaphysical ways in which Lord Narayana assists his devotees, there are also numerous mythological stories and legends that illustrate how he intervenes in their lives to overcome various challenges and obstacles.

One such story is the tale of Prahlada, a devout young prince who was a steadfast devotee of Lord Narayana. Despite facing persecution and oppression from his father, the demon king Hiranyakashipu, Prahlada remained unwavering in his devotion to Lord Narayana. In the face of adversity, Lord Narayana protected Prahlada from harm, ultimately appearing in the form of the half-man, half-lion incarnation known as Narasimha to destroy Hiranyakashipu and restore peace and righteousness to the world.

Another famous legend involving Lord Narayana is the story of Gajendra, the king of elephants, who found himself ensnared by a crocodile while bathing in a lake. Despite his immense strength, Gajendra was unable to free himself from the crocodile's grip. In his moment of desperation, Gajendra called out to Lord Narayana for help, offering a heartfelt prayer of surrender and devotion. Moved by Gajendra's sincere plea, Lord Narayana swiftly came to his rescue, slaying the crocodile and liberating Gajendra from his suffering.

These stories, and many others like them, serve as powerful reminders of Lord Narayana's boundless compassion and willingness to come to the aid of his devotees in times of need. Whether through divine intervention, miraculous manifestations, or acts of protection and guidance, Lord Narayana's love and grace are ever-present, offering solace, strength, and support to those who turn to him with faith and devotion.

IV

In Hindu mythology, Goddess Lakshmi is revered as the deity of wealth, prosperity, and abundance. Devotees believe that she possesses the power to bestow material and spiritual prosperity upon those who worship her with devotion and sincerity. One of the primary ways in which Goddess Lakshmi is believed to help everyone attain wealth and prosperity is through her blessings and grace. Devotees pray to her with reverence, seeking her blessings for success, prosperity, and financial stability in their lives. By cultivating a relationship with Goddess Lakshmi through prayer, worship, and acts of devotion, devotees believe that they can attract her divine blessings and favor.

Goddess Lakshmi is also associated with the concept of abundance and generosity. Devotees believe that by embodying the qualities of generosity, gratitude, and compassion in their own lives, they can align themselves with the energy of Goddess Lakshmi and attract wealth and prosperity into their lives. Acts of charity, kindness, and service are seen as ways to honor Goddess Lakshmi and invite her blessings into one's life.

Furthermore, Goddess Lakshmi is often depicted as being closely associated with Lord Vishnu, the preserver of the universe. Devotees believe that when they worship Goddess Lakshmi alongside Lord Vishnu, they invite both wealth and spiritual prosperity into their lives. This dual aspect of material and spiritual abundance is considered essential for holistic well-being and fulfillment.

In addition to her role as the bestower of wealth and prosperity, Goddess Lakshmi is also believed to symbolize qualities such as beauty, grace, and auspiciousness. Devotees adorn their homes and places of worship with images and symbols of Goddess Lakshmi during festivals and special occasions, seeking her blessings for prosperity and good fortune.

The ways in which Goddess Lakshmi helps everyone to attain wealth and prosperity are deeply rooted in the principles of devotion, gratitude, and generosity. By honoring her with reverence and cultivating a relationship with her through prayer and acts of devotion, devotees believe that they can attract her divine blessings and experience abundance in all aspects of their lives.

Lakshmi ji is reversed as the goddess of wealth, prosperity, and abundance, and she is believed to bring good fortune and blessings to her devotees. The relationships between Lakshmi and Narayan in considered to one of eternal love and devotion.

Lakshmi is often depicted as siting at the feet of Narayan or massaging his feet symbolizing her service and devotion to him.

She is said to be deeply devoted to Narayan and is always by his side supporting him in his role as the preserver and protector of the universe.

Lakshmi love for Narayan is unconditional and selfless and she is believed to embody the qualities of compassion, grace and abundance that flow from her deep connection with Narayan.

In Mahabharat; "in the Mahabharata an ancient Indian epic, there are references to Lakshmi as the consort of Vishnu and their divine love".

The love between Lakshmi and Narayan is seen as divine union that represents the harmonious balance famine and masculine energies in the universe. That's why the beauty of the universe increases so much never decreases.

Their relationship symbolizes the ideal of a loving and supportive partnership based on mutual respect, devotion and shared values.

Whoever keeps these things of love in their life, life gets happiness and prosperity along with good results in life.

Devotes of Lakshmi and Narayan often seek their blessing for prosperity, happiness and spiritual fulfillment in their lives. These are the rules of life and our nature; whatever you get back what you give them therefore, think a thousand times before harming others. Let's all live together in love and happiness.

Narayan is considered the preserves and protector of universe, and he is often depicted as embodying righteousness, wisdom and dharma (righteousness). It is believed that Narayan's actions are always guided by his divine knowledge and sense of duty.

While there are stories where Narayan takes on different form and roles to uphold dharma and protect the world, there are no specific instances in Hindu mythology where Narayan is portrayed as being "wrong" in his actions or decisions. As the supreme deity, Narayan is considered infallible and in is revered for his wisdom and divine nature.

However, in some stories, goddess Lakshmi, as the consort of Narayan is depicted as offering guidance, support and wisdom to her beloved Narayan. Lakshmi is seen as a source of divine grace and blessings, and her presence is believed to bring prosperity and abundance to the world.

While there may not be a specific story where Lakshmi corrects Narayanji's actions their relationship is often portrayed as one of mutual respect, love and devotions Lakshmi's role as the goddess of wealth and prosperity complements Narayan's role as the preserver of the universe, and together they embody the ideal of a harmonious partnership based on mutual support and shared values. Devotees of Lakshmi and Narayan seek their blessings for guidance, prosperity, and spiritual fulfillment in their lives.

V

Pandits are a prominent social class in Hindu society, traditionally regarded as priests and scholars. They are part of the Varna system in Hinduism, which categorizes society into four main groups based on occupation and duties. Pandits are typically associated with roles related to teaching, performing rituals, and upholding religious traditions.

Pandits are belonging to Brahmins culture places a strong emphasis on education, spirituality, and adherence to religious practices.

They are often seen as the intellectual and spiritual leaders of the community. Respect for elders, knowledge, and religious customs are key aspects of Brahmin culture.

In terms of family life, Pandits often follow traditional customs and values, placing importance on family unity, respect for elders, and maintaining religious traditions within the household. Marriage within the same caste is common in Brahmin families to preserve cultural and social traditions.

Pandits culture is deeply rooted in religious beliefs, education, and the preservation of customs and traditions passed down through generations. In traditional Brahmin culture, the wife of a Pundit man often dresses modestly and elegantly. The traditional attire for a Panditain that is the Brahmin woman typically includes a saree, which is a long piece of fabric draped around the body in a graceful manner. The saree is usually paired with traditional jewelry such as earrings, necklaces, bangles, and sometimes a bindi (a decorative mark worn on the forehead).

Panditain also often adorn themselves with sindoor, which is a red powder worn in the parting of the hair, and wear mehndi (henna) designs on their hands during special occasions.

The traditional look of a Panditain reflects cultural values, modesty, and elegance, emphasizing the importance of tradition and customs within Brahmin households.

In Brahmin culture, mutual respect between the husband and wife is highly valued. Both partners are expected to treat each other with respect, understanding,and consideration. Respect in Brahmin marriages is often based on traditional values of mutual support, trust, and honoring each other's roles within the family and society.

Husbands are expected to respect their wives' opinions, contributions to the household, and their role in maintaining family traditions. Similarly, wives are expected to respect their husbands' decisions, support them in their endeavors, and contribute to the well-being of the family.

Mutual respect forms the foundation of a harmonious relationship in Pundit families, where both partners work together to uphold cultural values, traditions, and the sanctity ofmarriage. In Brahmin marriages, both the husband and wife have distinct roles and responsibilities that are influenced by traditional values and cultural norms. The roles in Brahmin marriages are often defined by gender expectations and societal customs.

Husbands in Brahmin marriages are typically seen as the providers and protectors of the family. They are responsible for earning a living, ensuring the financial stability of the household, and making important decisions that affect the family. Husbands are also expected to uphold religious practices, pass down traditions, and provide emotional support to their wives and children.

Wives in Brahmin marriages often take on the role of homemakers and caretakers of the family. They are responsible for managing the household, taking care of children, preparing meals, and maintaining family traditions. Wives also play a significant role in upholding cultural practices, participating in religious ceremonies, and supporting their husbands in their endeavors.

The roles in Pundit marriages are based on a division of labor that reflects traditional gender roles and expectations within the community. While these roles may vary based on individual circumstances and modern influences, they are rooted in cultural values that emphasize harmony, mutual support, and the preservation of traditions.

In Brahmin culture, respect towards one's family is highly valued. Brahmin families often prioritize respect for elders, parents, and ancestors. Family members are expected to treat each other with reverence, consideration, and care.

Respect towards family in Brahmin households involves honoring family traditions, following cultural customs, and maintaining strong family bonds. Children are taught to respect their parents, grandparents, and other elders in the family. Elders, in turn, are respected for their wisdom, guidance, and experience.

Family gatherings, rituals, and celebrations are important occasions where respect towards family members is demonstrated through gestures of kindness, support, and love. Upholding family values, traditions, and unity are central to the concept of respect within Brahmin families.

They respect towards their family members is a fundamental aspect of Brahmin culture, fostering a sense of belonging, tradition, and interconnectedness within the family unit. If a Pundit or Panditain decides to marry against their family's wishes, they may encounter several consequences. Firstly, they might experience social ostracism, where they are excluded from family events and community gatherings. Additionally, there could be disapproval from the family, leading to strained relationships and emotional distress. Financial support might also be withdrawn, and there could be cultural and religious implications, affecting their acceptance within the community. The emotional impact of such a decision can be significant, causing inner conflict and turmoil. It's essential to navigate these challenges with communication and understanding to potentially rebuild relationships over time. In Brahmin culture, if someone chooses to marry against them family's wishes, they may face various consequences depending on the family's beliefs, traditions, and values. Marrying against the family's expectations can lead to strained relationships, social stigma, and disapproval from relatives and the community.

It's important to note that the consequences of marrying against the family can vary widely depending on the specific family dynamics, individual circumstances, and the level of traditional adherence within the Brahmin community. Communication, understanding, and eventual acceptance may help in resolving conflicts and rebuilding relationships over time.

A story that happened in some such survival A Pundit married a Pundit woman against the wishes of his family and the family members separated them both. Know the end of this story while facing a lot of problems both succeeded due to their faith and devotion and how did the god Narayanji grace fall upon them?

Once upon a time, there lived a Pundit and Panditain in a small village, both of them left home for the sake of love and worked hard to convince their umpire and now their condition was such that they were very rich by their hard work, struggling and grace of goddess Lakshmi and there was a lot of love between them due to the blessings of Narayanji.

They both separated from their families and worked very hard, they were very sad to be separated from their family.

They were happy to get happiness in their life due to their hard work, but there is still one worry about the happiness of their parents, they had to be free from this worry too. They also had such thoughts that how long would their hopes be able to move forward without the blessings of their elders.

Whatever has been achieved after so much hard work, there came a time when God thought of testing their devotion Lakshmi ji took away their wealth and Narayanji took away their house with the help of chakra storm. But there was such deep love and trust between them that they stood by each other firmly any moment and holding each other's hand.

Thinking of fighting their situation together, both of them started struggling in their lives and neither got along. Seeing their hard work and affection for each other, even God would be convinced that if love is true then they will be able to stay together no matter what will happen and how!

They get a lot of inspiration from all the sorrows but they learneda lot from everything, their parents were also shaken by all these incidents and after seeing their efforts, their parents also except them. Good, true and loving means always bear fruits.

At that time his and her parents also bless them and teach them that troubles and difficulties will always came at every turn and every situations, you will have to move ahead with faith in god and your biggest hard work. Then you definitely get the success.

After time, due to his hard work and dedication, he and she started becoming a little capable and their family members also decided to support them.

God was pleased with their love and returned their wealth and house, both of them pleased god with their love. In this way, we can remain with our true love by supporting and reliance each other in every difficult moment.

From all these things it is known that God also wanted them all to become one. Due to the devotion and faith of both of them, even god might not have wanted to keep them away from their parents, hence god created such a plan so that they can also meet and together with their family, may they also get love from their parents and like everyone else, they too should have a happy family. Maintaining a happy and healthy relationship with a spouse, especially when you're a Pundit, can involve several key aspects. Communication is super important; make sure to talk openly, listen actively, and be understanding of each other's perspectives.

Spending quality time together, whether it's going on dates, sharing hobbies, or simply having meaningful conversations, can strengthen your bond. Showing appreciation and gratitude for each other's efforts and qualities can go a long way in fostering a positive relationship. Also, it's crucial to support each other's goals and aspirations, both personally and professionally. Lastly, handling conflicts with patience, respect, and a willingness to compromise can help navigate challenges smoothly. Remember, every relationship is unique, so finding what works best for you and your spouse is key to a happy and enduring partnership.

Maintaining a healthy and problem-solving relationship with a Pundit and his wife, Panditain, requires a delicate balance of respect, communication, empathy, and cultural understanding. As pillars of their community, Pandits and their spouses often carry significant responsibilities, both religious and social, which can influence their interactions and dynamics with others. Therefore, fostering a positive and productive relationship with them involves navigating cultural nuances while fostering mutual respect and understanding.

At the core of this relationship lies respect - respect for their roles within the community, their knowledge, traditions, and values. Acknowledging and honoring their expertise in matters of spirituality and culture lays the groundwork for a relationship built on mutual admiration.

Demonstrating reverence for their contributions and the significance of their roles not only validates their identity but also sets a tone of appreciation within the relationship. Open and transparent communication serves as a cornerstone for maintaining a healthy rapport with Pandits and Panditains. Establishing a channel for dialogue where both parties feel heard and understood fosters trust and strengthens the bond between them. Whether discussing matters of religious significance, personal concerns, or day-to- dayinteractions, effective communication ensures that any potential misunderstandings are addressed promptly and constructively.

Empathy plays a crucial role in navigating the complexities of relationships with Pandits and Panditains.

Understanding the pressures and expectations they face within their community and the broader society can foster a deeper connection based on empathy and compassion. By putting themselves in their shoes, individuals can better appreciate the challenges they encounter and offer support and understanding when needed.

Collaboration is key in resolving conflicts and addressing challenges within the relationship. Approaching issues as a team, rather than placing blame or resorting to confrontation, promotes a sense of unity and shared responsibility. By working together to find mutually beneficial solutions, both parties can overcome obstacles and strengthen their bond in the process.

Respecting boundaries is essential in maintaining a healthy and respectful relationship with Pandits and Panditains. While it's important to engage with them and show interest in their lives and traditions, it's equally crucial to recognize and honor their personal space and privacy. Respecting their boundaries demonstrates consideration and reinforces trust within the relationship.

Cultural understanding is fundamental in navigating the intricacies of relationships with Pandits and Panditains. Educating oneself about their customs, beliefs, and traditions not only promotes mutual respect but also fosters a deeper connection based on shared values and experiences.

Embracing their cultural heritage and participating in their traditions can further strengthen the bond between individuals and foster a sense of belonging within the relationship.

In maintaining a healthy and problem-solving relationship with a Pundit and his wife, Panditain, requires a combination of respect, communication, empathy, collaboration, boundary- setting, and cultural understanding. By cultivating these qualities within the relationship, individuals can foster a connection based on mutual respect, understanding, and support, enriching their lives and communities in the process.

"If there is a desire to be fulfilled then one can fulfill it in any way, and God is there to help the true people to win"

In this fast-paced world, you will meet many people; good, bad, wrong, right, but 'keep in mind that you cannot make anyone happy, that's okay, but you shouldn't even think about hurting anyone is very big mistake'.

No one in this world has the right to hurt anyone, because everyone already has their own difficulties. If there is a lot of trouble in your life then is nothing to worry about it, this means that you are still unable to become as strong as you deserve to be. That's why god is still testing your strength and your level of stamina.

In this world no one suffers equally but everyone suffers.

What about us we are just human beings when god resided in these place even then there also happiness was accompanied by pain, pain was accompanied with comfort and peace was accompanied by sorrow.

Therefore, the relation between Pundit and Panditain are very much unanticipated deep affectionate love for each other, this love gave the strength to fight and tackle with every unexpected norm and situation.

After overcoming so many difficulties, both of them got the support of their families and are now living a happy life together.

Not all shortcomings are there at every turn of life, some happen and some remain, still work hard, sometime or the other there will definitely be shortcomings hard work makes everything easy if anything is done with true devotion, dedication and hard work, it will surely be successful. Nothing can be achieved without hard work so keep working hard.

"ARGUMENT-is the book is totally based on fictional mythology here is an argument between lord Narayana and the god of wealth Shree Lakshmiji and the faith of a Pandit family.

Rina Roy